ENDANGERED
Animals of the Sea

William B. Rice

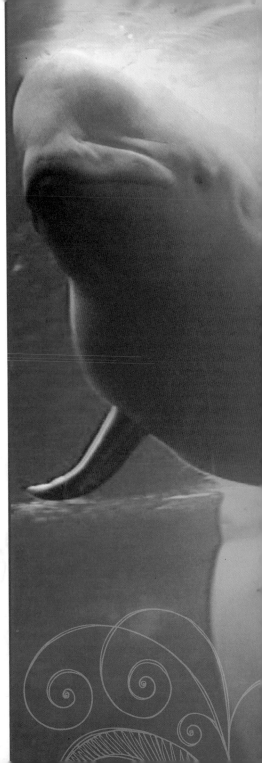

Consultants

Timothy Rasinski, Ph.D.
Kent State University

Lori Oczkus
Literacy Consultant

Thorsten Pape
Animal Trainer

Based on writing from
TIME For Kids. TIME For Kids and the *TIME For Kids* logo are registered trademarks of TIME Inc. Used under license.

Publishing Credits

Dona Herweck Rice, *Editor-in-Chief*
Lee Aucoin, *Creative Director*
Jamey Acosta, *Senior Editor*
Heidi Fiedler, *Editor*
Lexa Hoang, *Designer*
Stephanie Reid, *Photo Editor*
Rachelle Cracchiolo, *M.S.Ed., Publisher*

Teacher Created Materials

5301 Oceanus Drive
Huntington Beach, CA 92649-1030
http://www.tcmpub.com

ISBN 978-1-4333-4935-5

TABLE OF CONTENTS

A WORLD IN DANGER

Looking out across an ocean, beautiful colors can be seen over soft ripples in the water. It seems like an empty, peaceful world. But drop down, down, down, down to the ocean depths. Currents rush and swirl. The Earth shifts. And fish and mammals dart everywhere.

From the land and air above, we can't see these precious sea creatures. But they're there. And they need us to protect them. We must keep their world safe so they can live and grow strong. Together, we can make a difference.

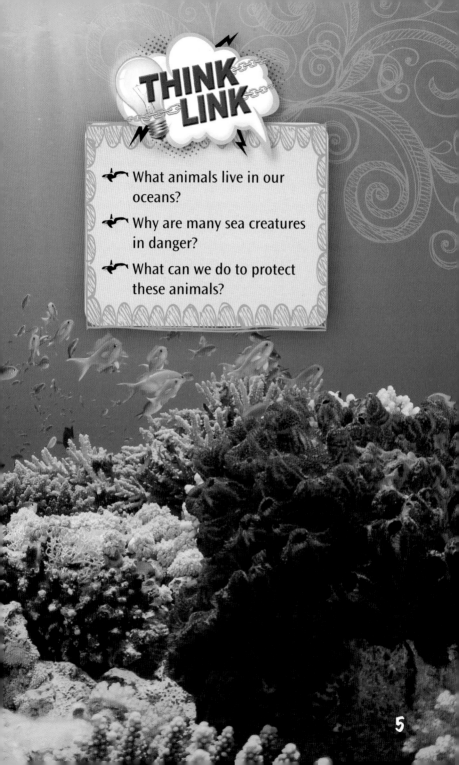

THINK LINK

- What animals live in our oceans?

- Why are many sea creatures in danger?

- What can we do to protect these animals?

Unfortunately, many ocean animals are not safe. They are **endangered**. They are in danger of being wiped out, gone from the planet forever.

Why? Some of it is just nature. **Species** come and go because of natural changes in life and the Earth. But more often, it's people who are at fault. People overfish. People **pollute** the water. And people destroy animal habitats without thinking about what the animals there need. Their actions are putting the entire planet in danger.

Garbage is filling our oceans and harming the animals that live in them.

Endangered

To be endangered is to be threatened and at risk of **extinction**, or being wiped out completely. Over time, many species have become extinct. But the good news is, with help, the numbers of some endangered species have grown larger.

Pollution

Oil spills, dumping trash, and excess chemicals all have terrible consequences on the health and well-being of life in the ocean—and all the rest of us, too. The largest trash dump in the world is in the middle of the North Pacific Ocean. The Great Pacific Garbage Patch is hundreds of miles across! Ocean currents make it a catchall for trash from around the world.

oil spilling from a rig

Overfishing is a good example of the "tragedy of the commons." This idea refers to a common resource shared by many people. The tragedy is when they overuse it. Not only do they lose it, but everyone who might one day use it does as well. If everyone works together to keep the resource in balance, it will be there to use forever.

Fishing is like that. Many fishers fish for food and profit. But if each thinks only about what he or she needs and doesn't think about fish replenishing themselves, then a species can be wiped out. Then, that fisher and all fishers lose out. And so do the people and other sea life that eat the fish.

Garrett Hardin, an American ecologist who wrote about the dangers of overpopulation, first wrote an essay titled "The Tragedy of the Commons" in the late 1960s.

A small boat takes a small amount of the fish.

Another small boat takes its share of the fish.

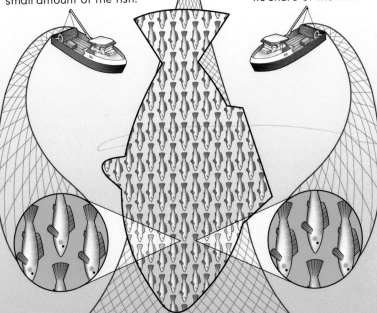

A small loss of fish may not do any harm on its own. But when many boats take their own small share, it can add up to too many fish.

TOTAL RESOURCES USED

Will the Fish Survive?

How does overfishing work? Imagine there are 1,000,000 bluestar trout in the ocean and 100 fishers. Each fisher catches 1,000 bluestars each year. The bluestars **reproduce** at the rate of 10 percent of the total population each year before they are caught.

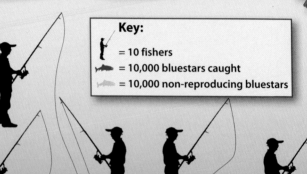

Key:

= 10 fishers

= 10,000 bluestars caught

= 10,000 non-reproducing bluestars

STOP! THINK...

Note: Bluestar trout is not a real species, and the numbers in this equation are not real, either. But the diagram does show how overfishing can lead to extinction.

- Will the bluestars survive this year?
- What if the fishers caught more fish or less?
- How can the fishers share the fish so everyone thrives?

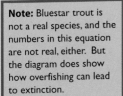

Answer: The bluestar trout will survive but are right at the edge of overfishing. The fishers catch fish at the same rate the fish reproduce. If the fishers catch more fish, the bluestar's will eventually be extinct. If they catch less fish, the population will increase over time. But other sea life may catch and eat the bluestar, too—and that may move the bluestar beyond the rate of survival.

PACIFIC OCEAN

As the largest ocean, the Pacific covers approximately a third of Earth's surface. Countless marine plants and animals call it home. However, sea creatures are at risk no matter where they live. Those in the Pacific Ocean are no exception.

Chinook Salmon

Chinook salmon are usually bluish-green, with some silver and white on their sides and belly. As they age, they may turn a color somewhere between copper and deep red. The males develop a hooked upper lip and a big ridge along their backs. The chinook salmon is a popular fish to eat. It is endangered due to overfishing and changes to or loss of **habitat**.

Adult chinook salmon can range between 3 and 5 feet long and weigh between 40 and 120 pounds.

During spawning season, female chinook salmon dig big holes or nests called *redds* in sandy river bottoms where they lay their eggs.

Coming Full Circle

Chinook salmon, like many fish, are **anadromous**. This means they are born in a freshwater river or stream. During their first year, they swim downstream, eating and growing bigger. Eventually, they make their way to the ocean where they live most of their lives. At the end of their lives, they return to the freshwater river or stream where they were born. They **spawn**, lay their eggs, and die.

SEA OTTERS

Sea otters are related to weasels. Their thick, dark fur, which keeps them warm in the ocean, is the thickest fur of any animal on Earth. Sea otters have broad, flat webbed hind feet, which help them swim in the water. But walking on land is difficult. They are playful, social animals, but still spend a lot of their time alone.

They may be cute, but otters are still in danger. Otters are endangered mainly because they have been hunted for their fur. Oil pollution, poaching, and fishing equipment are also threats to otters.

Anchors Away

Otters can be seen floating in large patches of seaweed. They twist their legs through the vines and sleep peacefully, knowing the seaweed will keep them from floating away from the other otters.

Sea otters are marine mammals. Adults usually grow to between 30 to 100 pounds and 3 to 5 feet long.

On the Way Back

Sea otters were nearly hunted to extinction. But worldwide **conservation** efforts and hunting laws have helped them make a strong recovery. Their recovery is thought to be one of the greatest successes in marine conservation.

Female Steller sea lions usually grow to around nine feet long and may weigh over 700 pounds. Males are much larger, growing up to 11 feet long and weighing up to 2,500 pounds.

STELLER SEA LION

Steller sea lions are endangered. But the causes for this are not fully known. Some scientists think the fish they eat have been overfished. Others think pollution and climate change may be factors.

Adult Steller sea lions are pale yellow or reddish. The males have bigger, broader heads than females and more fur around their large thick necks. That makes them look like they have a mane.

Hunted

In the past, people hunted sea lions for their meat, blubber, and skin. Their skin was used to make boats. Today, killing Steller sea lions is against the law in the United States, Canada, and Russia.

Andean Catfish

The Andean catfish is a small freshwater fish that lives in the rivers and streams of the Ecuadoran Andes Mountains. They are critically endangered from overfishing, habitat loss, and pollution. The catfish can find food in the dark by using the barbels, which look like whiskers, around their mouths.

BOCACCIO ROCKFISH

Bocaccio rockfish are critically endangered due to overfishing and being caught as **bycatch**. They are found in many different colors, including dark green, bright orange, brown, and light bronze. Bocaccio are called *rockfish* because they mainly live among rocks on the bottom of the ocean. Protecting their homes may be one way to help them survive.

jaw

Bocaccio is an Italian word that means "big mouth." These fish are named for their famously long jaws.

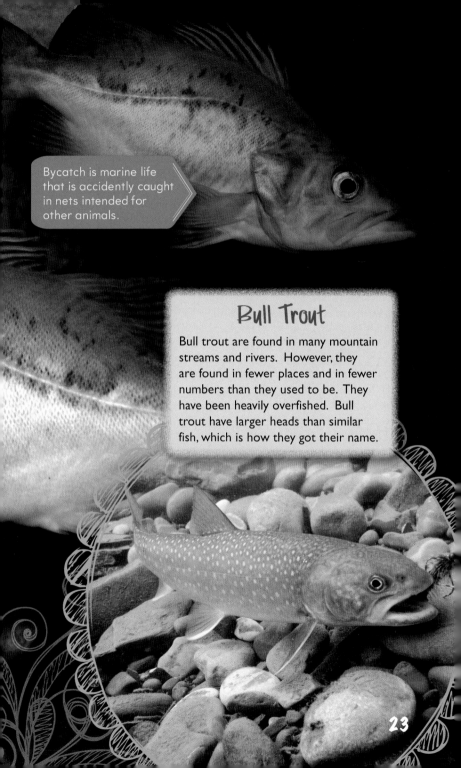

Bycatch is marine life that is accidently caught in nets intended for other animals.

Bull Trout

Bull trout are found in many mountain streams and rivers. However, they are found in fewer places and in fewer numbers than they used to be. They have been heavily overfished. Bull trout have larger heads than similar fish, which is how they got their name.

ATLANTIC OCEAN

The Atlantic Ocean is one of the most popular fishing sites in the world. It is home to a variety of unique sea creatures. Due to the Atlantic's **abundance** of fisheries, many marine species are endangered as a result of overfishing.

Atlantic Bluefin Tuna

Atlantic bluefin tuna is a highly prized fish that is endangered as a result of overfishing. A healthy bluefin can grow to nearly 1,000 pounds! Bluefin are native to the Atlantic Ocean and the Mediterranean Sea, but they have been **extirpated** from the Black Sea, or made extinct in that area.

ATLANTIC COD

Atlantic cod mainly live along the bottom of the shallower depths of the ocean. Cod were popular to eat for many decades. But the **fishery** collapsed in the early 1990s. Overfishing and technology destroyed the ecosystem and caused the collapse. Fishing for cod was outlawed. But the number of cod has not **recovered**.

Cod can grow over 50 inches long and weigh up to 75 pounds.

How the Mighty Have Fallen

The Atlantic cod was an **apex predator** at the top of the food chain. Overfishing of the cod significantly disrupted the food web and other fish took its place.

ATLANTIC GOLIATH GROUPER

The Atlantic goliath grouper is endangered from overfishing. It lives mainly in shallow, tropical waters. Sometimes, it is found along the New England coast.

Grouper are considered very tasty. That's one big reason for their endangered status—people like to eat them. Another cause can be found in their own nature. Goliath grouper are curious and fearless. Those qualities can get them into trouble and probably contribute to their endangerment.

Beluga Sturgeon

The beluga sturgeon is a freshwater fish that is endangered from overfishing and **poaching**. It is found mainly in the Caspian and Black Seas and occasionally in the Adriatic Sea. It is one of the largest fish on Earth. In the past, it was mainly caught for the female's eggs. The eggs, or *caviar*, have been a highly prized **delicacy**.

Grouper are big eaters. They eat crabs, lobsters, shrimp, other fish, octopuses, and even young sea turtles.

Grouper can grow over 8 feet long and weigh more than 800 pounds!

SMALLTOOTH SAWFISH

Remember the movie *Finding Nemo*? Dory, Nemo, and a school of fish all get trapped in a giant fishing net. They work together and free themselves. The smalltooth sawfish isn't so lucky or clever. Getting caught in fishing nets is a serious danger.

The smalltooth sawfish is found in shallow tropical waters. It can grow up to 25 feet long. Sawfish are related to sharks and rays. They have long snouts with a row of sharp teeth along each side. They use their teeth to catch other sea animals for food.

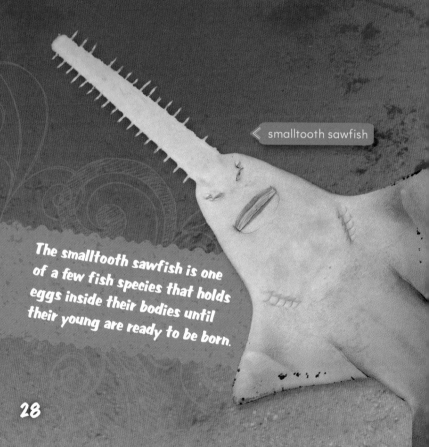

smalltooth sawfish

The smalltooth sawfish is one of a few fish species that holds eggs inside their bodies until their young are ready to be born.

28

Angel sharks have an unusually flat body that makes them resemble rays.

Not Your Typical Shark

Angel sharks are a large group of fish that includes endangered and critically endangered species. Different species can be found in many parts of the world's oceans. They are endangered because of overfishing and low reproductive rates.

STAGHORN CORAL

Staghorn coral is beautiful. It is also critically endangered. Outbreaks of disease and **coral bleaching** are two main causes for this.

The coral is found in many places but most famously in the Great Barrier Reef. Staghorn coral colonies look like the antlers of a male deer. The colonies can grow up to six feet tall and six feet wide. Many other sea animals live with and among the coral and coral reefs.

Great Barrier Reef

The Great Barrier Reef is a coral-reef system off the coast of Australia. It covers 135,000 miles of the Coral Sea, making it the largest coral-reef system in the world. The reef is made by small organisms called *coral polyps*. The Great Barrier Reef Marine Park helps protect the reef from damage, preserving it for future generations of people and animals.

Coral Bleaching

Coral and algae live together in a close relationship and depend on each other to live. The algae actually live inside the small individual coral animals. Sometimes, the algae may leave the coral, which causes coral bleaching, or the loss of color. The algae leave for many reasons, including changes in water temperatures, increased acid in the water, increased soil particles from land, and chemical pollution.

Coral reefs form important underwater environments.

EUROPEAN EEL

The European eel is a snake-like fish. It is endangered by many factors, including overfishing, **parasites**, and pollution.

European eels hatch from eggs in the ocean. Larvae float in the ocean for about 300 days. As young eels, they swim upstream in freshwater rivers and streams. They are clear, making them look like tiny glass eels. They may live for 5 to 20 years in freshwater. Then, as adults, they swim back downstream to the ocean to mate and lay their eggs.

New Numbers

The European eel is disappearing. Scientists have observed 99 percent fewer eels in the Atlantic Ocean than previously seen.

European eels usually grow up to two to three feet long, but in some cases have been known to grow to nearly five feet long.

For many years, eels have been an important food source. Jellied eels are a well-known food in England.

33

DIG DEEPER!

Elusive Eels

The more marine biologists know about sea animals, the better they can protect them. But there is still much to learn. No one has been able to find the eels' breeding grounds. Experts think European eels may mate in the Sargasso Sea. Until they know more, it will be difficult to protect them.

Currents carry the eggs from the ocean to freshwater rivers and streams.

SARGASSO SEA

Eels lay their eggs somewhere in the Sargasso Sea.

Adult eels travel back into the ocean 30 or 40 years later to breed again.

Different Dangers

Animals that live in many different places face many different threats. Ocean waters are warming, which changes the ocean currents. Some spots are ripe for catching eels to use as food. Other eels may be trapped by dry rivers or water dams as they migrate.

The eel is just one example of an animal we need to know more about before we can better protect it.

INDIAN OCEAN

During an underwater tour of the Indian Ocean, you might see gigantic sea turtles or tiny, brightly colored reef fish. But the beautiful and fascinating marine life of the Indian Ocean is in trouble, too. Why? The reasons are much the same as elsewhere. And the help needed for these creatures is much the same, too.

Big Fish!

The Mekong giant catfish is critically endangered from overfishing, habitat destruction, and pollution. It is the largest freshwater fish on the planet.

Weighing in at 644 pounds, this is the largest freshwater fish ever found.

GIANT CLAM

Giant clams are in high demand. People want to eat them, and they want their shells for decoration. As the name suggests, giant clams are the largest-known living **bivalve**. Bivalve animals live inside two hard shells that open and close together.

Giant clams attach themselves to the sea floor and don't move. They depend on a type of algae that lives in the clam's skin. The algae give the clam nutrients. The clam provides nutrients and a safe place for the algae to live.

Giant clams are found in the shallow coral reefs of the Indian Ocean and South Pacific Ocean.

How giant is giant? These clams can grow to more than 4 feet across and weigh over 400 pounds.

DUGONG

Like dolphins and otters, dugongs are sea mammals. They mainly eat sea grasses. The grasses are found on the ocean bottom in shallow coastal areas. Dugongs have been hunted for thousands of years for their meat and the oil from their blubber.

Dugongs live long lives. One is known to have lived 73 years. There are few sea animals that prey on the dugong. But crocodiles, orca, and sharks may eat their young.

Most countries have outlawed hunting dugongs. But they are still at risk. This is due to pollution, habitat destruction, and boating accidents. The dugong also reproduces slowly.

Manatee or Mermaid?

Manatees look a lot like dugongs but are a different species. They once could be found in many places, but they are endangered now for the same reasons as dugongs. Because of their appearance when surfacing at sea, they are likely the source of stories about mermaids.

Dugongs and manatees are sometimes called sea cows. That's because they graze on sea grass in the same way that cows graze on grass on land.

AROUND THE WORLD

A **cosmopolitan** species can be found in many places throughout all or most of the world. Such a species is comfortable in many locations. But their flexibility doesn't always keep them safe. Many of these species are endangered, too.

Physical Pollution

Physical pollution causes problems for leatherback sea turtles because they may eat trash, such as balloons and plastic bags, that look like the leatherback's favorite food, jellyfish. In their stomachs and intestines, the trash can keep the turtles from absorbing food or block it from going through the digestive system.

LEATHERBACK SEA TURTLE

The leatherback sea turtle is the largest of all sea turtles. It doesn't have a hard, bony shell like other turtles. Instead, its shell is made of skin and oily flesh, similar to leather.

Leatherback turtles have a teardrop-shaped body, which enables them to move through the water faster and easier than any other turtle can. They mainly eat jellyfish, which helps keep jellyfish populations in check.

The leatherback is critically endangered because its eggs have been harvested for food. Many indirect factors, such as being caught as bycatch and pollution, have also harmed it.

Hawksbill Turtle

The hawksbill turtle, which gets its name from its curved beak, is endangered for many reasons, including hunting, poaching, and habitat destruction. Many people like the taste of hawksbill sea turtles and consider them a delicacy. Hawksbills also have beautiful shells and people harvest their shells for jewelry, brushes, combs, rings, and other decorations.

LOGGERHEAD SEA TURTLE

Female sea turtles lay their eggs in a nest in the sand on their nesting beaches. But the loggerhead sea turtle is losing its nesting beaches. Fewer places to nest means fewer babies. The loggerhead is also often caught in fishing equipment and hunted by exotic predators. All these factors have led to the turtle's endangerment.

Chemical Pollution

Dangerous levels of harmful chemicals have been found in the eggs of some sea turtles, which may affect the development of the babies.

Sea turtles are reptiles just like tortoises, snakes, and lizards.

Feeding

Loggerheads eat many different kinds of sea creatures, including sea snails, clams, crabs, and lobsters. They have very large, powerful jaws that help them break open the shells of their food.

BLUE WHALE

Blue whales are endangered mainly because of hunting. Many were killed during the early 1900s. Most hunting stopped by the 1970s, but their numbers still have not recovered. Whales may also get tangled in fishing equipment and be sickened by water pollution.

Blue whales are the largest living animals on Earth. In fact, there has probably never been a larger animal on Earth. Blue whales are long, slender, and colored in different shades of gray and blue. We are only just beginning to learn how intelligent they may be.

A crowd surrounds a whale stranded off the coast of France in 1904.

Whale Hunting

People have hunted whales for thousands of years. In the past, people caught whales for food and for the oil in the whale's blubber. Businesses have been **banned** from hunting whales since the 1970s. However, some native peoples are still allowed to catch enough whales to live on.

Blue whales have been found up to 108 feet long and may weigh up to 330,000 pounds.

Chow Down

Blue whales are baleen whales, which means they have many stiff, bristly plates in their mouths instead of teeth. They use baleen to filter food from seawater. Blue whales mainly eat krill, which are small sea animals similar to shrimp. Blue whales may eat up to 7,900 pounds of krill a day.

Scientists remove a piece of baleen from a whale that washed up dead onto the beach.

SPERM WHALE

Sperm whales have the largest brain of any animal on Earth. Their name comes from the substance that is found in their head. It is called *spermaceti*. It is milky white in color and has a waxy texture.

Sperm whales were once hunted mainly for their spermaceti, which was used for candles, soap, cosmetics, and machine oil. They were also hunted for their ambergris, which was used to make perfumes. Ambergris is a gray, solid, waxy substance. It is found in the whale's digestive system.

Hunting in the past caused the sperm whale's population to dwindle. The whales are also often caught in fishing nets, and sometimes they collide with ships.

Big Guys

Male sperm whales can grow up to 52 feet long and weigh up to 45 tons. Sperm whales usually dive down 1,000 to 3,000 feet, but they have been known to dive down as far as 9,800 feet, farther than any mammal does.

spermaceti
processing plant
in the 1950s

Wondering Why

Scientists don't know
why sperm whales make
spermaceti. They think it may
help the whales dive up and
down through the water more
easily, but they aren't sure.

Sperm whales eat
many different kinds
of sea animals, but
mainly they eat squid,
octopuses, and rays.

WHALE SHARK

The whale shark is found in tropical waters and is the largest shark in the world. Despite their threatening size, whale sharks don't have big teeth for catching and chomping their food. They are **filter feeders**. They swim around collecting small sea organisms in their big mouths and then filter out the water through their gills. Whale sharks are a common type of seafood, and that has made them endangered.

Whale sharks are colored gray, with a white belly and yellow spots and stripes on their backs.

Whale sharks can grow to more than 40 feet long and weigh more than 21 tons.

Whale sharks are very calm, gentle animals and have been known to allow underwater divers to hitch rides on their backs.

Truly Tropical

Whale sharks live in all tropical waters. Every spring, they migrate to the west coast of Australia.

What a Waste

Sometimes, natural changes in the environment threaten fish. Other times, overfishing causes fish populations to decline. People need food to eat, and people are hungry for fish. But other times, the need is unclear.

Shark finning is a brutal practice in which a shark's fin is cut off to be used in traditional medicines and soups. The rest of the shark goes unused and is thrown back into the ocean to drown or bleed to death.

The spermaceti in sperm whales nearly brought these mammoth creatures to extinction. The spermaceti organ holds as much as 530 gallons of spermaceti. It was used to light oil lamps and make candles. The whale meat was an afterthought.

The hawksbill turtle is hunted for its shell. The elaborate patterns on the shells are polished and used for decorations and jewelry.

GREAT WHITE SHARK

The great white shark is vulnerable. Hunters catch them for food and sport. They have several rows of large teeth that are prized as trophies. Their teeth also make them excellent meat eaters. They eat fish, dolphins, seals, sea turtles, otters, and even seabirds. The great white shark is one of the most dangerous sharks in the world. But little is known about the lives of these sharks. That makes it hard to protect them.

Many sharks have serrated teeth, which means the teeth have sharp, jagged edges like a saw.

Sixth Sense

Like other sharks, great whites have an extra sense. They use their ampullae (am-PUHL-uh) of Lorenzini to learn about the world. The ampullae form a network of receptors around the shark's head. They sense very weak electrical fields and small temperature differences in the water. All sea animals have an electrical field. The ampullae help sharks track nearby animals.

These sharks have a light gray back and a white belly.

COME TOGETHER

Ocean animals around the world are being threatened. Pollution, overfishing, loss of habitat, and other human activities are putting these creatures in danger. But by studying them and learning what they need to survive, we can protect them. If everyone works together, we can make a difference.

David Suzuki Foundation

SOLUTIONS ARE IN OUR NATURE

SeaChoice.org
for healthy oceans

FISH WISE

Help Out

Talk with your family about organizations (such as those above) that work to protect the ocean and help threatened and endangered marine life recover. Contact these organizations to see how you can help.

So what can YOU do?

Protect the Environment

Always remember the three Rs— **reduce, reuse, and recycle.** Practicing the three Rs goes a long way in helping the environment and animal species.

Protect Habitats

Don't pollute the oceans— remember, they are home to billions of sea creatures.

Making a Difference

Many people around the world are working to protect endangered species and their environments. Some were early heroes of the movement. Others are still leading the way today. Learn who they are—and maybe you will want to join them, too!

Carl Safina

Carl Safina is passionate about the ocean. He has written several books on the topic and founded the environmental organization Blue Ocean Institute. Safina believes people and nature have an inseparable relationship. He teaches others to care for the Earth's oceans and ocean life.

Jacques Cousteau

Jacques Cousteau was famous throughout most of his adult life as a passionate ocean explorer and eventually an ocean activist. His development of the Aqua-Lung, which is a pioneering piece of SCUBA equipment, as well as his many ocean documentary movies helped pave the way for ocean exploration and understanding. Cousteau's passion about the ocean led to his fierce concern to protect it. Today, his granddaughter Alexandra continues his work.

Sylvia Earle

Known as "The Sturgeon General" and "Her Deepness," Sylvia Earle is a longtime advocate for ocean conservation. She is a past chief-scientist with the National Oceanic and Atmospheric Administration. *TIME* magazine once named her a Hero for the Planet. Earle is committed to ocean exploration and research.

The Birch Aquarium

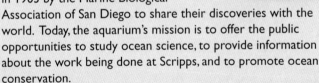

The Birch Aquarium is located at the Scripps Institute of Oceanography at the University of California, San Diego. The aquarium was named in honor of Stephen and Mary Birch's support. Each year, more than 400,000 people visit the aquarium. The original aquarium was founded in 1903 by the Marine Biological Association of San Diego to share their discoveries with the world. Today, the aquarium's mission is to offer the public opportunities to study ocean science, to provide information about the work being done at Scripps, and to promote ocean conservation.

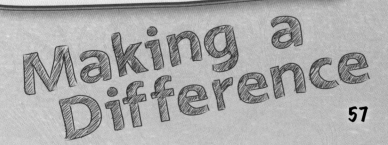

Making a Difference

GLOSSARY

abundance—an overflowing or fullness of a certain quantity

anadromous—born in freshwater, swims to and lives in the ocean, and returns to its birthplace to spawn, lay eggs, and die

apex predator—the creature at the top of the food chain

banned—not allowed by legal means

bivalve—having two hard shells that open and close together

bycatch—marine life that is caught by accident in nets or fishing equipment intended for other marine life

conservation—the protection of plant and animal species and the environment

coral bleaching—the dangerous loss of algae in coral, resulting in the loss of color

cosmopolitan—found around the world

delicacy—something pleasing to eat because it is rare or a luxury

ecologist—a person who specializes in and studies the science of how living things relate to their environment

ecosystem—all the plants, animals, and other elements of a particular area

endangered—threatened and at risk of extinction

extinction—the complete elimination of a species from

extirpated—extinct within a local area while still existing elsewhere

exotic—very different or unusual

filter feeders—animals that get their food from water that passes through their systems

fishery—an area of the ocean where a specific type of fish is caught by people using specific equipment

habitat—a natural living environment

parasites—organisms that live and feed off other animals without providing anything in return or immediately killing the animal

poaching—hunting or fishing illegally, usually for some financial gain

pollute—to release high amounts of a chemical or waste into the environment

population—the organisms occupying an area

recovered—returned to a healthy and sustainable condition

reproduce—to make offspring

spawn—to deposit or fertilize eggs in the water

species—a specific animal group with common characteristics

INDEX

BIBLIOGRAPHY

Bradley, Timothy. *Demons of the Deep.*
Teacher Created Materials, 2013.

Learn about some of the strange sea creatures scientists are finding in the deepest layers of the sea. Many are already endangered.

Kalman, Bobbie. *Endangered Sea Turtles.*
Crabtree Publishing Company, 2004.

Learn more about the endangered sea turtle. You'll learn more than just why they are endangered—you'll learn about their anatomy, life cycle, behavior, and how people are helping to protect them.

Kurlansky, Mark. *World Without Fish.*
Workman Publishing Company, 2011.

What is happening to the world's fish population? This former commercial fisherman will teach you about the fish that may become extinct and what you can do to keep that from happening.

Wyland, Robert. *Learn to Draw and Paint with Wyland.*
Walter Foster, 2002.

Make a difference helping endangered sea animals like Wyland does. This book will teach you drawing and painting techniques that can improve your skills and help endangered animals at the same time. You can create posters and flyers to bring more attention to the endangered animals of the sea.

MORE TO EXPLORE

Endangered Animals Game!

http://www.sheppardsoftware.com/content/animals/kidscorner/
endangered_animals/endangered_game.htm

You will learn more about endangered animals around the world while playing this interactive game. Earn bonus points by clicking the crane and correctly answering the questions. Answer all the questions correctly, and you and the animals will be rewarded with a special surprise!

Protecting the Ocean

http://ocean.nationalgeographic.com/ocean/protect

Here, you will see lots of beautiful photographs of animals and their habitats that need your help. Each picture also includes a paragraph about the animal and how it became endangered.

Especies Fact Sheets

http://www.kidsplanet.org/factsheets/map.html

Get the facts about endangered species from around the world. This site has an extensive list of animals that are in danger. Search the list by continent, name, or habitat. Each animal on the list has a fact sheet, status of protection, and additional links for more information. You will also learn about the Endangered Species Act and why it is important.

Our Endangered Animals

http://www.konicaminolta.com/kids/endangered_animals/comics/index.html

Why are animals in trouble, and how can we help? Follow Hiroto and Miki through this seven-part comic as they explain different reasons endangered animals are in trouble.

ABOUT THE AUTHOR

William B. Rice grew up in Pomona, California, and graduated from Idaho State University with a degree in geology. He works at a California state agency that strives to protect the quality of surface and groundwater resources. Protecting and preserving the environment is important to him. William is married with two children and lives in Southern California.